Moving Forward

Moving Forward

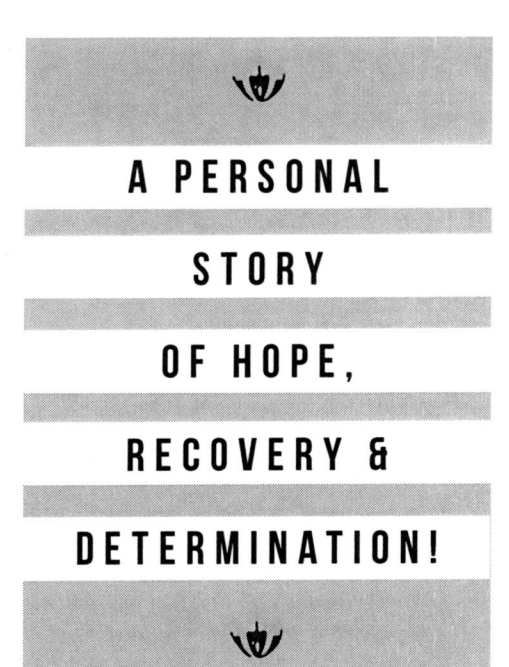

A PERSONAL STORY OF HOPE, RECOVERY & DETERMINATION!

WAYNE P. GILLIS

Copyright © 2013 Wayne P. Gillis.

Certain interior images reprinted with permission from The Halifax Herald Limited

All rights reserved. No part of this book may be used or reproduced by any means, graphic, electronic, or mechanical, including photocopying, recording, taping or by any information storage retrieval system without the written permission of the publisher except in the case of brief quotations embodied in critical articles and reviews.

Balboa Press books may be ordered through booksellers or by contacting:

Balboa Press
A Division of Hay House
1663 Liberty Drive
Bloomington, IN 47403
www.balboapress.com
1-(877) 407-4847

Because of the dynamic nature of the Internet, any web addresses or links contained in this book may have changed since publication and may no longer be valid. The views expressed in this work are solely those of the author and do not necessarily reflect the views of the publisher, and the publisher hereby disclaims any responsibility for them.

The author of this book does not dispense medical advice or prescribe the use of any technique as a form of treatment for physical, emotional, or medical problems without the advice of a physician, either directly or indirectly. The intent of the author is only to offer information of a general nature to help you in your quest for emotional and spiritual well-being. In the event you use any of the information in this book for yourself, which is your constitutional right, the author and the publisher assume no responsibility for your actions.

Any people depicted in stock imagery provided by Thinkstock are models, and such images are being used for illustrative purposes only.
Certain stock imagery © Thinkstock.

Printed in the United States of America

ISBN: 978-1-4525-6782-2 (sc)
ISBN: 978-1-4525-6783-9 (e)

Library of Congress Control Number: 2013902127

Balboa Press rev. date: 4/1/2013

CONTENTS

Preface
/vii

Acknowledgments
/ix

Note to the Reader
/xi

Chapter 1: Ready, Set, Go
/1

Chapter 2: Daily Activities
/11

Chapter 3: Barriers and Obstacles
/19

Chapter 4: Growing Up & Lifestyle Direction
/27

Chapter 5: Emotional Roller Coaster
/35

Chapter 6: Adaptations
/41

Chapter 7: Finding Self-Worth
/51

Chapter 8: Being Proud
/57

Chapter 9: Reflection and Choices
/63

Chapter 10: Hold On to the Hope
/67

Chapter 11: Attaining Peace
/71

Epilogue
/75

Appendix A
/83

Appendix B
/85

Preface

My theory applies to each and every thought and experience that we are involved in, and it provides the foundation for our "energy source." Setting high goals and then exceeding them can be an unrealistic approach to reality; however, setting realistic goals and then achieving them gives you the opportunity to reach your goal, feel proud, and then reevaluate the situation. You can then adapt and set a new goal to focus all your attention and energy on. Following humans' unique and adaptive nature, this attitude allows us to adjust our actions accordingly and continue to move on. Over the past seven-plus years of my life, I have learned that perspective is everything! Here is mine.

Acknowledgments

Special thanks to everyone who assisted me in writing this book and to those I've made special connections with; especially Kiki-Sauriol-Roode, Michael Zareski, Roy Leffell, Justin Hayes & photographer Christine Heinz for her family and Author photo. However most importantly, to my father and deceased mother.

Atop all of these are my wife and children. They've been with me through all my ebbs and flows, my ups and downs, and, most of all, my ever-changing lifestyle regime to stay in balance. I thank them with all my heart!

Please excuse any typos, misprints or word confusion as rebuilding who I once was is still full of daily tests! For any noticed, I apologize.

NOTE TO THE READER

I hope that writing my experiences down on paper in the form of this book will help others to gain value from this information. Looking quickly online, one can find ample thoughts and blogs about head injuries. In fact, head and brain trauma represent a significantly large sample size of personal injury. An Occupational Therapist I saw refers to them as the 'invisible disability'. This is something I can personally attest to because through society's eyes, I look very 'normal'.

I hope the information found in my book will help people not only achieve what they choose to achieve in life, but also identify the things they cannot do or the things that require too much effort to do now. The choice of what goals to pursue is unique to the individual, and finding balance in a person's physical and mental game is the real source of one's satisfaction. The dictionary defines *hope* as "the feeling that what is wanted can be had or that events will turn out for the best" (www.dictionary.com)[1]. It is this hope that fosters my desire for continued improvement, with total recovery as the final outcome. Having the hope to reach this outcome is an admirable quality, but actively walking this path is a real experience one can always adapt to.

---

1 Dictionary.com OnLine, s.v. "hope" accessed Jan 18, 2013 http://dictionary.reference.com/browse/hope?s=t

CHAPTER 1:

READY, SET, GO

On September 7, 2005, I experienced a life-changing event. I am not a born-again Christian per se, but I have been given a second chance at this game called life. On that day, I was involved in a severe automobile collision when a car struck the motorcycle I was driving. I suffered numerous physical injuries, including seven broken ribs, a ruptured spleen, a bruised liver, a torn bowel, fourth cranial nerve damage, (hence the double vision), and a bilateral pneumothorax, or two punctured lungs; however, the most dramatic and life-altering injury was the closed-head traumatic brain injury (TBI) I received. I was unconscious at the scene, so my number on the Glasgow Coma Scale from 3 to 15 was simply a 3. (See the neuropsychological paraphrase in the Appendix A.)

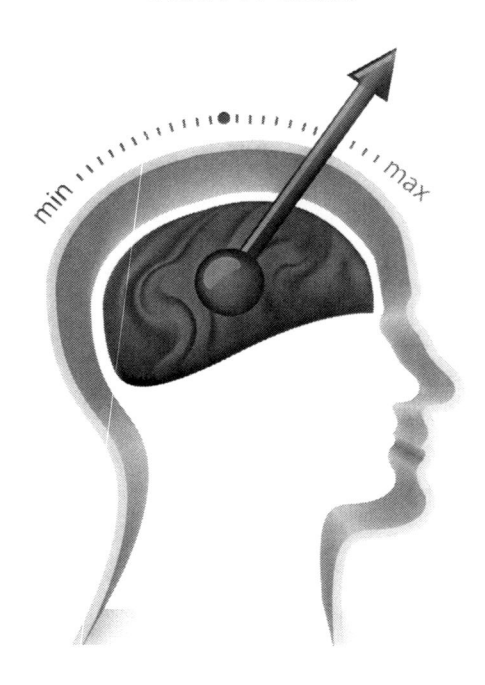

When looking at the severity of my injury, my mother-in-law, a board-certified doctor in urgent care, jokingly commented, "By scoring that low, one simply shows up for the test, but no one is home." Therefore, when one is a 3 on the Glasgow Coma Scale, one is simply alive! I was not breathing at the scene, but somehow I was still fighting or being safeguarded in a way. However having an off duty paramedic at the accident site on other business and him establishing an airway for me, enhances the reason for my survival! This again focuses me towards sharing this info with others so they can find real direction in their life as it was this injury that started my life over again! In the early stages of my recovery, I sent an e-mail to a select group of individuals whose perspectives on my abilities and character gave me better clarity regarding the reality of who I was and how I acted.

Unfortunately my brain, like the hard drive of a computer, became fragmented, with all of the data disbursed throughout it. In an attempt to rebuild the neural pathways that had become misdirected, I sent out the following email request to begin rebuilding the life that was taken away from me. I did this with hopes to adapt to the barriers & obstacles now placed before me.

> *"Just a quick note as I'm attempting to make a list of things other people like or find interesting in me. In an attempt to create a positive self-image, I will use this list whenever I'm feeling down or whenever I hear critical voices in my head leading me down the negative path. Unfortunately the accident I was involved in leaves me little characteristics of myself that are self-assuring to me. I need to find myself before and I find balance with others in my life.*
>
> *I sent this list to those I want to hear from that represent the best-balanced group I had. Rest assured, I use the blind carbon copy BCC format so your e-mail address will not be forwarded.*
>
> *Wayne*
>
> *PS. I could ask each of you this question but having a paper copy of your comments gives me something to reflect on in times of need."*

To my enlightenment, the responses I received were very fulfilling, and even to this day, I reflect on them when moments of weakness arrive. This practice has helped me on my journey as a brain injury survivor. In comparison to what my neurosurgeon indicated, injuries like this on outgoing and extroverted personalities such as mine, prove very challenging for those individuals to handle. Unfortunately, that comparison is difficult for these individuals to realize, and they must develop new ways of life to achieve their desired outcomes. In my early discussions with the vocational counselor at the Nova Scotia Rehabilitation Hospital, he gave me a new term to use. In my discussions with him, I often said that I now had to "react to certain situations." It was then that he said, "Instead of the word *react*, use the word *adapt*. Instead of reacting to a situation, adapt and find a new way to formulate the end result." This way of thinking provides a proactive approach to attaining the desired outcome, instead of a reaction to something that is outside of your control. Approaching life this way provides you with personal ownership and accountability for your actions, and it's more productive than reacting to things outside of your influence. As a result of this revelation, the website www.always-adapt.com was born!

Several weeks into my recovery, I became aware of my situation and faced the reality of my injury. According to the Centers for Disease Control and Prevention,

> Traumatic brain injury (TBI) is a serious public health problem in the United States. Each year, traumatic brain injuries contribute to a substantial number of deaths and cases of permanent disability. Recent data shows that, on average, approximately 1.7 million people sustain a traumatic brain injury annually. (http://www.cdc.gov/traumaticbraininjury/)

In my case, I too share this disability level. Fortunately for me, mine is a disability that has improved considerably over time. It is this improvement that feeds the hope I have and the energy I would like to share with others by writing this book. Before we begin, you need to have an understanding of a few definitions. People like Anthony Robbins and Jim Rhone provide others with the *motivation* to pursue a goal.

Recently I took a trip to Toronto, Ontario, to see Dr. Wayne Dyer at the "I Can Do It!" conference, and he revealed that he considers himself an *inspirational* speaker, not a motivational one. It is my hope that by providing this information, I too can help people achieve their goals—not through motivation or inspiration but through *determination*. People can be motivated or inspired to follow a path, but if they are not *determined* to achieve what they choose to do, they will fall short of the desired outcome. Using motivational or inspirational tools to achieve what you choose to do provides a solid foundation for your energy source. This energy source follows the same guidelines that the universe uses, as Esther Hicks points out in her book *The Vortex*. It is this law of attraction that responds to everything!

Occasionally, as I look through the self-help folder I established for myself, which contains the returned e-mails from my previous thoughts I sent out to people, a response from one individual stands out. He noted that, based on all of the information concerning my accident, I had been given another "opportunity to live this life." That e-mail in particular holds a lot of value for me. All the other responses that came back to me identified certain features of my character; this was the one response that stood out in terms of content. This response spoke of one's physical memory, the functioning of one's life, and the conduct of one's relationship with others.

The next level of memory assists in solving problems that we encounter from time to time, and of course the deeper levels of memory are where we tap into ourselves and ask such philosophical questions as "Why am I here?" and "What is the purpose of life?"

From his e-mail response, I quote the following:

> Memory is not all in the mind or in the brain. As you go through your exercises, you will come to appreciate that it is in every cell of your body. Your blood cells remember how to re-create themselves as blood cells, and your skin cells, bone cells, and muscle cells operate the same way. Your thoughts and experiences create the memories of who you are and pave the way for who you will become.

It is here that this gentleman refers to the fact that I have been given a whole new opportunity to play this game called life, create a whole new Wayne Gillis and build a new life unfettered by old memories.

However, he advises me,

> Take time to go within to get in touch with your inner subconscious, and keep in contact with your angels and guides, as they are there to help you with everything that you do. This in the eternal present and know that you are exactly where you have to be on your journey through life.

Here we see an example of a religious belief (i.e., angels). Religious beliefs, like scientific ones, are arguably debatable. It is not my intent to debate beliefs or facts, however; it is my intent to identify the singularity that exists within both themes. As the universe will decide on everything that it has created or that exists in its realm, my choice is to focus on the energy source that has created everything.

This energy source depends on what country you are born in, as it is defined by the people around you and the god of their choice. Christianity, Islam, Buddhism, and all other capital-R religions—each represents organized faith and requires discipline to follow the guidelines determined by each. In Christianity, we see in the Bible that God created man in his own image; however, it could be argued, with the multitude of religions available, that man created God in his image. It is this same focus, or style of energy, that is displayed on the television show *Long Island Medium*, which emphasizes the religious experience over the scientific route. On this show, the star of the series has the ability to communicate with people who have crossed over to the other side after death.

Once they have left the physical world they remain intact, and through her, they can communicate quite powerfully and specifically to the person who engages this star's special gift. Addressing specific details that only the person being communicated to would know eliminates any chance of her simply guessing the details of this or that event. With my personal views and with this information watched on television, the spiritual belief gains significant weight in the religion/science debate. Religions differ geographically and the energy received from this gathering of information is spiritual in nature. However, since most religions share a similar belief system, they reflect for me the 'source energy' the universe has.

Again, people similar to Anthony Robbins, Jim Rhone, and Zig Ziegler give people the motivation to pursue their dreams. From my own personal standpoint, and the past seven years of my life, I understand intimately that you have to be motivated to do something and inspired to pursue that direction, but, ultimately, achieving a goal comes down to the individual's choice to do it. No matter how motivated you are, how inspired you become, or what scientific or religious beliefs you have, you must be personally determined to succeed! By adapting to what is delivered your way, you're no longer reacting; you are proactively redirecting your focus to attain the desired outcome.

Looking back, over the past seven years, at the barriers that presented themselves to me, my hope and determination to achieve a desired outcome has always helped me maintain a positive outlook towards my improvement. Like my neurosurgeon told me in a discussion early on, it is not that people choose to plateau with their recovery. By having the upper cognitive ability to think and digest information, one can always keep the hope for improvement alive. I am very thankful that I do have the upper level of thought to fuel my rehabilitation process and keep the slope positive! For me, I have always held on to the hope, as it is this absolute that leads different individuals to achieve different results and levels of success.

What causes one individual with devastating lifestyle injuries to heal better than someone else with similar injuries? If the person has that cognitive option, it ultimately boils down to his or her ability to choose to continue to recover. It is here—through this choice—that we see different levels of cognitive adaptation, ultimately determining what an individual is able to achieve. Now being the active participant, instead of simply just the spectator, we have a choice. Since we technically only use 20 percent of our brain, hopefully establishing new neural pathways to find a solution to the problem can be achieved. By choosing to 'adapt' to an obstacle we can turn a 'deficit' into a short term 'deficiency' so that by continuing to 'Move Forward' we are still in the race!

ULTIMATELY, we see that having the ability to make the choice is the real difference. No matter how motivated you are or how inspired you become, the reality is that your ability to achieve your goals boils down to your choice! I have learned that to make this choice, you have to be determined to do so. According to Dr. Wayne Dyer's book *Excuses Be Gone*, one must *choose*, not *excuse*. On occasion, I say that to my wife—jokingly, of course!

As you gather information by reading books and hearing lectures, you start to transform your intellect into knowledge. I believe that intellect plus knowledge equals wisdom. By seeing where I was and feeling where I am now, I truly believe that I am a very good representation of a determined person. You can look to Anthony Robbins for motivation, Dr. Wayne Dyer for inspiration, and Wayne Gillis for determination!

CHAPTER 2:

Daily Activities

I BELIEVE THAT OUR daily activities are broken down based on our environment. Individually, if we are responsible only for ourselves on an independent level, we foster selfish choices. We may consider other people's opinions when making choices, but fundamentally we act based on our own individual choice. When other people's opinions are involved in our choices (i.e., in a romantic relationship or when dealing with children), the same choices are no longer selfish; they are of a selfless nature.

Up until my accident, I had successfully obtained several jobs in which I performed well, but after a decade of being good at a handful of jobs, I wanted to become very good at one thing or find a career. Because I was good with my hands, I thought I could attain a job relating to something mechanical—like a mechanical engineer. On that note, and following my desire to use a scientific approach toward things, I went back to university to earn a bachelor of science degree. This was the start for me in attaining my desired career as a mechanic of the human body—a doctor.

Participating in the academic environment that university offered, I took the basic science and math courses: chemistry, biology, physics, and calculus. Those are the fundamental courses required for a Bachelor of Science degree; however, I needed something to major in. My strong rapport in the physics field led me down that path; however, my weakness in math proved disheartening. Growing up, I had a strong association with religious beliefs, and having this foundation of spiritualism reduced my scientific approach to education. This upbringing fostered a reduction in the scientific approach to life but did not eliminate it for me. However to better balance my university experience, I took courses like Philosophy and English.

However, after taking introductory psychology, I felt a better balance in my lifestyle equation. It was this course that changed my direction and led me to a major in psychology. Psychology, unlike Philosophy and English courses, provided me with a better understanding of the lifestyle game we all play. Understanding the physical sciences like chemistry and biology gave me a better understanding of our scientific nature. However adding psychology to this equation gave me a more balanced approach to the process of life and a healthier understanding of how the mind works. At my university, a preset number of courses were needed to declare a major, in addition to a group of electives, as they were called. In an effort to find the lifestyle path I wanted to be on, I took a psychology course dedicated to the psychology of law.

It was then that my lifestyle path changed once again—toward a future in law. My past roles in the financial industry gave me strong verbal fluency, which supported my pursuit of becoming a litigator. Unfortunately, as I was actively involved in the process of completing my science degree, with hopes to eventually enter law school, my accident occurred.

While I returned to school, my wife supported my academic venture by working part-time. She made the choice to work part-time because we were involved in raising a family while I was going to school. Since her time was limited because of her maternal role, her effort to support my academic journey was limited too. On September 7, 2005, however, she received a phone call from the Royal Canadian Mounted Police, telling her that her husband had been involved in motor-vehicle collision and that she needed to get to the hospital as soon as she could. At that time, our youngest son was four months old. After she collected her thoughts and prioritized her commitments, our neighbor took her to the hospital. Making her way to the hospital to verify my condition with her own eyes, she chose, as difficult as it was, to think positively about my situation, but she felt deflated upon arriving at hospital. Once there, she was asked to wait in a designated family room to speak to the doctor responsible for my care.

She discussed the situation with the doctor; I was to be kept in a medically induced coma in order to keep my intercranial brain pressure (ICP) down until I physically recovered to where I needed to be. At that point, I was fed a liquid diet via a hose that went up my nose and down into my stomach. At some point, the medicine that induced the coma would be stopped so that my body could take care of itself. The force of trauma resulted in injuries to my brain, and, like a sprained thumb, my brain began to swell. To relieve this pressure, and because mine was a closed-head injury, a hole was drilled in my skull. Like opening a can of soda, this hole offset the pressure that was building up from the swelling and bleeding.

However, my ICP would spike at times as a result of the audible contact from people visiting and talking to me. This was reassuring to those close by my side, as it helped them feel hopeful for my recovery. The collision had caused my motorcycle to collide with the passenger side of the pickup truck, so the impact my head experienced was on the left side, therefore effecting my right side motor control; the left side of your brain controls the right side of your body. Accordingly to a past physics instructor of mine, based on the speed I was traveling and my weight, the force of the impact was like falling headfirst off a seven-story building! After four weeks, my vital signs improved, and the medical team felt that I could be taken off the medication. I would then wake up, and my body's natural healing state would take over.

My family waited anxiously for my revival to consciousness, but, sadly, it did not happen the next day. Since the trauma I'd received was so severe, "further time was needed," according to the medical team monitoring my recovery, but still the next day I did not wake up. On the third day, a resident doctor spoke to my family about the situation and said she was surprised that even though I was showing all the physical signs of waking up, I was not. She thought the problem was perhaps oxygen deprivation, as I had not been breathing at the scene of the accident; she told my family that my current state might be "as good as it gets." After my family heard that information, their thoughts played games with their reasoning, and worst-case scenarios played out in their minds. As horrifying as it must have been, with the same optimistic mind-set she'd shown throughout the entire process, my wife asked to speak to the head neurosurgeon responsible for my care. At that time, the medical team's advice was to remove the life support that was sustaining my life energy. However, her response was crystal clear and without a shadow of a doubt: a perfectly healthy and resilient person like I was needed more than just four days to recover!

The head neurosurgeon said that in his thirty-five years performing in that job, he had never seen someone show all the physical signs of alert consciousness without waking up. He too was surprised at my condition. Having my wife's unwavering support and possibly hearing the doctor's words on a subconscious level, the next day I woke up (see the following news video: http://youtu.be/GmGijhz_Oro).

AT the beginning of my recovery, I acted more like a spectator in life's game than an active participant. I was functioning, but only at a basic level. My wife had legal power of attorney over me and was making all the necessary decisions regarding my condition and my care. Not only was she dealing with the fear of the unknown, but she was also raising two young boys and always holding on to the hope for my continued recovery. Once again we see the positive energy that my wife chose to give off whenever in my presence. It is the same positive energy that she ensured all visitors gave off as well, making my place of recovery that much more suitable to the forward motion I write of.

Emotions play a detailed part in processing our thoughts, and it was through her emotions that my wife gave off her real energy. Holding true to an optimistic and positive outlook, she gave me the subconscious energy I used for my recovery and for my continued improvement. I'm sure feelings played a detailed part in my wife's lifestyle direction, and her ability to distance herself from the possibilities of what could be provided me with the hope I needed. It was this positive energy source that helped me greatly in my recovery. I have these words by my computer workstation, which I saw at a local exercise gym that reads as follows:

> By changing your thinking, you change your beliefs. When you change your beliefs, change your expectations. When you change your expectations, you change your attitude. When you change your attitude, you change your behavior. When you change your behavior, you change your performance. When you change your performance, you change your LIFE!

Following this guideline gave my wife the inner guidance she needed for being on the front line of this lifestyle event. Independently one can choose events that dictate the direction he or she moves in; however, interdependently one relies on the support of others who are meaningful in his or her life. I describe this comparison as either making a selfish choice or a selfless one.

FORTUNATE for me, my wife's selfless energy carried my entire family in the forward direction and helped them continue on this path. I was fortunate enough to regain the level of consciousness needed to individually be able to choose for myself. After being a spectator in life's game, I was now an active participant and was better able to choose what direction to follow.

Through the use of notes and reminders, I began to function not only as the father figure I was, but also as the husband my wife needed me to be. As she was endeavoring to retrain herself in an academically challenging veterinary career, having the lifestyle we chose to have, assistance in achieving this was a group-sensitive commitment. With my help, she could put 100 percent of her commitment toward reaching the status of DVM. However, her lifestyle equation was different from most students', for she had children and a husband to consider.

One would think that these types of extra variables would make the journey on an academic path more difficult. However, these variables add to the life experiences everyone attains, and using these experiences as information stepping-stones, one can find value in each choice he or she makes. For us, no question, I have learned that together we WE ARE stronger!

CHAPTER 3:

BARRIERS AND OBSTACLES

As with any lifestyle direction change, certain challenges occur with head and brain injuries. To begin with, the physical limitations of an injury like mine need to be addressed. The biggest lifestyle curveball is forgetfulness. Through the use of reminders, Post-it notes, and phone calls, overcoming this challenge begins.

We drove our eldest son to and from school, and on several occasions, I forgot to pick him up, so he started calling from the school phone to remind me to do so. When it was identified that I had forgotten to pick him up, at that time I did my best to focus on the positive aspects of the situation, and by doing so, I was able to realize the benefits I had. I was not bedridden or confined to a wheelchair, and I was not how I used to be—unconscious. I was physically able to drive, so picking him up was a reality. It just so happened that, in that case, I had forgotten.

At that time, my cognitive level was such that I was not drawn into the "negative vortex of energy," as Esther Hicks calls it, as I was simply life's watcher. However, now over seven years later, I find that the better I get, the harder it becomes to adapt. I sometimes make it harder by raising the bar too high and being tough on myself, by not cutting myself some slack or taking it easy on myself. However, I do find that by collecting my thoughts and transposing them into this book, I feel a sense of purpose. It is this feeling that carries the hope and gives me that meaningful feeling and the contentment I seek.

With regard to memory, we have both short-term and long-term memory banks. As it stands, my short-term memory banks were compromised, but my long-term memory banks remained intact. It is this short-term memory that causes me irritation, as it offers up-front and direct association with the current moment. My long-term memory was not affected, so focusing on that helped the deficiencies with my short-term memory bank. Like an affirmation I used to have printed and posted on my refrigerator, no matter how bad you think you have it, it can always be worse. No matter how the cards of life are dealt to you, it is all happening perfectly! Much easier said than done, but, nonetheless, this humble phrase reveals greatness in its straightforwardness and the energy it creates.

Learning to live a life with the use of refreshers and reminders can be difficult but it's an effective way to deal with the deficiencies of one's lifestyle in the event of memory lapses. Added to the "brain game" as I call it, is the physical one. When my upper level started improving, I wanted to focus my time, effort, and energy on the physical one. Since one's brain absorbs so much energy just to function, it is here I encountered another road block on my path. My brain was not only attempting to function but was also attempting to recover.

By establishing new neural pathways and establishing new ways information can follow energy is depleted. It is this reduction that causes the physical rehabilitative process to be very challenging. Simply throwing a Frisbee outside with my sons causes me physical concern as I am not as mobile as I once was. This is much better than being in a wheelchair but it still makes me feel physically limited.

However in comparison to very early in my recovery, having mobility at this level is amazing! When put in perspective, being physically able to perform at this level overshadows the level I once was in. Practicing basketball, playing catch and trying a golf drive are other avenues of activity that I tried. Unfortunately I attempted these activities before my vision was corrected through the binocular fusion surgeries. Therefore I attempted these activities with input and data from only one eye. Vision from the other eye was eliminated via a fogged-out covering on my glasses. This eliminated the diplopia or double vision, I had, but it also eradicated my depth perception!

Depth perception is needed in catching a Frisbee or a baseball or driving a golf ball off the tee. Since humans have binocular vision, having input from only one eye proved challenging; I had definition but not accuracy. Data from both the left and right eye gives one the true benefit of this vision. The strabismus surgery did not need to produce 100% binocular fusion as the brain can adjust accordingly. The brain can blend a twisted object-image disorder or misalignment of 5% or lower resulting in normal vision. So indeed, being physically able to function when your son requests that you play with him is a reward quite easily forgotten or discounted by something else. As time went on and after two strabismus surgeries, I regained binocular fusion. Having full vision again was a wonderful thing; however it was reduced some by the other physical deficits I had. I have learned that to use the term *deficit* in my situation is not appropriate. A deficit is something one cannot perform; however, in my case, deficits that were adapted to were simply *deficiencies* waiting for solutions.

To balance out any lifestyle situation and through the 'Law of Attraction' the mental aspect of recovery draws in or attracts the physical side. It is this corporal area, for the noticeable recovery I have already shown, is of high importance to me! When one starts life over like I have, a new appreciation for the physical flow or movement is understood. When one learns to walk again, this process establishes a unique perspective on mobility. It is this perspective that needs to be discussed further to paint a better picture of myself aimed at the 'Moving Forward' theme I talk about!

Upon regaining consciousness I simply acted like a newborn child. However, gratefully enough, I began to improve and once my upper awareness came into play, thoughtful adaptation came as well. It is this thoughtful adaptation and my genetic character that empowered the slope of my improvement to steadily increase. Having such an accelerated rate of progress surprised all of those around me, especially the medical team! Information gathered online shows ample avenues of material directing attention to a 'traumatic brain injury' and a large number of them reveal a very grim and depressing scene for the victim and family.

However, through a directed and focused rehabilitation team at the local healthcare authority, I started my journey on this 'lifestyle path'. Once I was physically ready and with their dedication, commitment and professionalism, my physio, speech and occupational therapy began a couple months after my accident. As seen in Appendix B on the last line, when I first arrived at the rehabilitation Hospital, tests to determine my motor control and communication level were conducted; out of a possible 56 points, I only managed 4!

To physically learn to sit up in bed, to having a body-lift style of crane move me into a wheelchair, gave me some mobility having somebody push me from location to location. On his daily visits and staying true to his form, my father would take me on exploring excursions as he pushed my wheelchair throughout the downtown area. Even in the dead of the winter with snow covered streets and sidewalks, his energy radiated my way. Through the same dedication and commitment, I too began moving forward on the path to total recovery and thank him lovingly for his effort!

With the hospital's physiotherapy team I began rebuilding the physical state that I once had. Through my daily routine of therapy, I started independent movement in a wheel chair then I fortunately regained enough motor control and strength to use a walker. By continuing to push the level of myself, I advanced into walking with simply a cane, then removing it completely to move somewhat naturally. Going through this rehabilitation process, I often tried to distance myself from the team's effort by saying "I'm too tired to continue" However a lady physiotherapist responsible for my immediate physical care, persistently kept me moving; moving forward no less! They counteracted my aloofness with the same energy they gave me throughout my entire stay at the hospital. However during my early recovery and to add some comedy to this experience, one morning I made my way to the shower area outside of my room under my own body control without the walker that assisted me.

Upon getting there I realized I walked without the assistance of the walker and quickly went back to my room to get it; I then proceeded to go and bathe accordingly. Nonetheless the entire time an on-duty nurse visualized this effort of mine. She saw me going to the shower unassisted without my walker and then saw me come back to my room to get it so I could go to the shower area appropriately! This indeed brought some amusement to the situation as I believe laughter and humor are positive particulars that feeds ones energy source in a beneficial and constructive way.

A few years into my recovery in a brief discussion during my yearly psychiatrist visit with Dr. Brenda Joyce, I was able to pat myself on the back. For all of the deficits and deficiencies I was plagued with but eventually overcame, it was her comment that energized my batteries. When my appointment ended and I was leaving, the discussion of collecting my thoughts and writing a book came into play. It was then that Brenda told me that my adaptive ability in overcoming my challenges and finding new ways to complete desired tasks was inspiring to her! Her perspective in this field is significant to me, and it was very reassuring and motivating to get that helpful feeling I desired.

As I left the appointment and said good-bye with a small hug, she said that it was too bad that our appointments only happened once per year because she really looked forward to them. I am very grateful that I am able to give that kind of feeling to another person, as it is this helpful nature that I find value in. As well, it is this helpful nature that I hope by sharing my story with others, will make a difference in someone's life.

As the energy of the universe controls everything, I believe that by channeling my energy outward to others, it will be absorbed and used accordingly. It is just like we learn in an entry-level physics course: energy cannot be destroyed; it can only change shape. By adapting to this change, one can take a proactive step in the direction his or her life is going. It is here we see a relation to one of the overall themes of this book: by keeping the slope positive and fundamentally continuing to adapt, we keep our direction 'Always Moving Forward'! ☺

CHAPTER 4:

GROWING UP & LIFESTYLE DIRECTION

Now that I have achieved status as an active participant in life's game, a reevaluation of my role needs to be determined. With my wife actively pursuing a role in veterinary medicine, and having two children, it is my turn to adapt accordingly. In a society where gender roles hold some social weight, becoming the stay-at-home dad—or the Mr. Mom, or whatever hat is worn—the emotional roller coaster begins. Past conversations with individuals fostering a similar gender-role reversal added value to my thoughts, including discussions about my psychiatrist's own personal life journey.

Traditional beliefs about the family unit stereotype the mother's and father's roles, so changing these roles isolates the family some, especially the parents. It is this isolation and lack of support from society that create the emotional roller coaster.

However, by staying true to yourself and focusing on the support of your family's needs, you can justify this role reversal as the better choice! My psychiatrist chose to do her residency later in life, after she had started her family. In essence, her husband, like me, fostered a similar motherly role, and he too felt societal pressure in this reversal. However, she has now moved past the GP designation to a specialized psychiatrist's role, so again like me, her husband's efforts allowed her to achieve her career goals. For every action, there is a reaction, and now she has—or, better yet, they have—moved further up society's financial ladder. It is here, through an interchange of society's feelings, one can see the true definition of inner peace. The increase in one's salary correlates directly to the increase in the father's time available to spend with his kids. Childhood is an especially important time, as when children grow up, there will come a time when they do not want to spend time with Dad, especially during puberty!

When a person is growing up, especially during a festive time like Christmas, ads on TV and other marketing materials push one's inner desire to obtain materialistic things. This desire is a learned behavior that gets influenced from the outside, and it leads to the misconception that obtaining these items and feeling this excitement results in happiness. Here we see, even at a young age, the power that marketing and advertising have in relation to our lifestyle balance. The anticipation of receiving a major department store's "wish book" for gift ideas at Christmas time is truly a heartfelt and genuine feeling all children have. Upon receiving this catalog, the young mind becomes directed toward receiving certain materialistic things. Here we see that society's influence is a real factor in determining our overall mental state of mind and that by associating these materialistic items with our inner feelings, we are led to believe that excitement equals happiness. Excitement relates to happiness, as most things that are exciting give us happy moments; however, the two terms are not the same.

I grew up with a very modest lifestyle, and receiving this catalog offered me a truly euphoric state. This mind-set continued during my young-adult life and followed me to my university years, when credit cards became part of my lifestyle. As a student in university, credit cards were easily approved. The credit card companies granted me seven of the seven credit cards I applied for. Information about income level was not needed in the approval of these credit cards—just simple confirmation that I was a current student. On that note, the "buy now, pay later" theme began! Compared to the modest lifestyle I had growing up, my new lifestyle, where items could be purchased on credit, gave me an increased level of social confidence wanted by everyone. This social confidence in fact was a false reality, as I did not have the financial worthiness for these credit cards; however, as part of the social game called life, I was approved for all seven of them.

Businesses use aggressive marketing campaigns to try to increase sales, but it is this same type of advertisement that can aggressively affect one's choices. The feeling is similar to riding up the track of a roller coaster, slowly getting to the top, cresting the peak, and then free-falling down the ride! One's choices made in excitement during moments of weakness may in hindsight be unfitting to one's lifestyle path.

Logically, it is easy to see that ultimately we create our choice; however, as our brain is composed of a logical side and an emotional side, our emotions can kick in. It is this same lifestyle condition that follows us through our entire lives. An advertising campaign full of promotional strategy can certainly affect our choice to buy or not to buy. Therefore, with the introduction of credit cards, this choice is made much easier, simply requiring a small portion of the total charged be paid—plus, of course, their prime directive of interest! Through my experience, I learned a fundamental rule of behavior that we all must appreciate and understand: people must keenly live within their means. In my early days at Canadian Imperial Bank of Commerce's telephone banking center, the bank's target of generating sales was a key ingredient for business growth. Debt-consolidation loans were considered a beneficial sale to a customer who had several credit cards that had high interest rates charged on their balances. With this loan, one could have a lower interest rate and, therefore, a lower payment, allowing for more disposable cash flow each month.

However, a new challenge existed: although the credit cards were now paid off, a new monthly loan payment was necessary. Unfortunately, the credit cards were never revoked from the customer, so he or she was free to use them again at his or her disposable. After time, the debt-consolidation loan payment was paid monthly in addition to new credit card payments. Therefore, this increase snowballed over time until the customer had an after-tax cash outflow far outside his or her total debt service ratio (TDSR), or payment zone.

If in fact history does repeat itself, the purpose of this book is to identify the simplicity of removing yourself from the entourage of society. As George Carlin said, in an interview in Venice, California, on Dec 17, 2007 by Henry Colman & Jenni Matz, in 1992 he chose to "divorce society." In simplistic terms, he was cutting off society's energy force or influence in his daily lifestyle choices and merely observing the activities as a true spectator. By observing these activities, one can digest the information received and use the data gathered to better his or her experiences and make new choices.

This comment supports further discussions, and quite possibly future themes of other material I will choose to write about. In relation to this current theme although seriously injured, I must continue to move forward and discuss the lifestyle challenges that exist.

In adapting as necessary, we see that no matter what cards life deals you, the poker game continues. It is this continuation of the game called life that truly needs to be felt by everyone. All marketing and society aside, reaching the end point of this journey should never truly be the goal. By remaining optimistic, true, and sincere, people can see that the true reward of life's game is the journey! By experiencing this game called life, individuals can truly find appreciation and respect for all the experiences they've had and can find the level of happiness they seek. It may not be true happiness they find; however, they receive a better understanding of their lifestyle.

As we talk about 'lifestyle direction', it is this phrase that needs to be clarified, as one needs to be able to make a cognitive choice in this regard. This effort ensures one's motion or path is in the right direction. Tuesdays and Thursdays are the two days of the week when I worked on drafting this manuscript, with the weekend following to edit. As part of a selfless lifestyle, one cannot choose an independent path but must choose an interdependent one.

TODAY being Thursday, I followed my routine practice and prepared to work on my manuscript; however, I had to attend to other duties first. Because of lifestyle commitments of my wife, her level of activity performing simple housekeeping tasks was diminished. So before I could actively work on drafting my manuscript, I needed to undertake these household duties. This is a good example of the lifestyle interdependency that comes with having a wife, children, and pets; there are other commitments one must perform before the independent, selfish activities can be fulfilled. Performing these activities shows one firsthand the interwoven commitments one has walking on this family path.

These lifestyle commitments are beneficial to me, as time sensitive as they may be; they provide me with not an immediate reward but an overall lifestyle one—one that I choose to feel. By simply taking one hour to perform the job at hand, I now feel a greater sense of well-being and gratitude while engaging my manuscript draft. The only thing that is real is the *now*; the choice one can ultimately make is how to react to any given situation. In conversations with people, their thoughts, their logic, and even their body language can formulate their opinions on something. Others' opinions are outside of one's control, and as the saying goes "it is none of your business what other people's opinions are." The only thing inside your control is your own personal reaction to something.

We see that the lifestyle direction one chooses to be a part of is full of ebbs and flows, pros and cons, or pluses and minuses. These fluctuations and our ability to adapt to them directs our journey toward achieving the lifestyle we desire. Making the choice to hold on to the positive aspect of a result, even though it is not your desired outcome, allows you the benefit of gaining positive energy from it and learning from your past actions. We see this level of learning begin at a young age as a baby crawls around, learns his or her body movements, and then examines and collects info on everything that comes to pass. Here we see the benefits of making a mistake or an incorrect choice, and similar to my discussions with my eldest son during his gymnastics training, we are learning to succeed by failing.

❦

ULTIMATELY, having negativity in our lives—or, as Esther Hicks calls it, contrast—we learn to "close the gap between the things that are so right in our life, and our current perspective about it."[2] Once we begin to look in the lifestyle direction of what we want, instead of focusing our energy on what we don't want, we will feel better. This relates to the saying she said as well, "a feeling is simply a thought we keep thinking."[2] Ultimately, if we have negative thoughts, we will feel bad. If we have positive thoughts about what an outcome may be, no matter how small, we will feel good. This in turn passes on positive energy in relation to this hopeful thought. By holding on to the hope, we supersede what science and logic determine to be the outcome. This thought was echoed during my last appointment with the neurosurgeon I was seeing at the time; he told me to "always hold on to the hope."

---

[2] Esther & Jerry Hicks, The Teachings of Abraham: *The Vortex* (USA, Hay House Inc., 2009) A CD accompany to this book.

CHAPTER 5:

EMOTIONAL ROLLER COASTER

As quoted by my psychiatrist, the "brain game is much tougher than the physical one you have done so well at." The mental aspects of one's recovery require more time and cognitive therapy in order for continued improvement. This therapy needs to be administered early in one's recovery, as this needs to be focused on before new neural pathways resulting in misdirection are established. These are much more difficult to recover from then the simple time sensitive, physical injuries, i.e. broken bones. I am very grateful that I did indeed have exceptional and brilliant heath care coverage from the Health Authority at my local hospital. After regaining consciousness and becoming more alert, it was here that my emotional challenge started!

The challenge of being emotionally compromised is a very difficult behavior to adapt to, especially when outside influences or stimuli are present. One lifestyle challenge created by being the father of two young boys is seen when a reprimand is given. From their young perspective, how serious is a comment I make when I demonstrate a contradictory action—for example, giving a reprimand while laughing? Unfortunately for me, saying, "No, you can't do that," and following it with a laugh doesn't hold much weight. It is here that I find my negative thoughts start to escalate themselves into negative feelings, and these negative feelings in turn affect my behavior and, ultimately, my choice. As with any adaptation in life, I am thankful for this negative energy, because it provides me with future clarity in making another choice. Again, like I tell my eldest son when he is competing in gymnastics, to accomplish a goal or achieve a desired move, you have to make mistakes. Unfortunately, you learn to succeed through failing, and by always operating outside of your comfort zone, you increase the probability of achieving a desired outcome. But you also increase the number of errors you make!

By never stepping or reaching outside of this comfort zone, individuals never grow. They may become excellent at what they do by performing the routine to perfection; however, by challenging themselves and performing outside the box, they choose to better themselves in hopes of achieving an overall improved outcome. When this outcome is reached, they can then choose a new direction or avenue to keep the slope positive. By having the cognitive ability to do so and the verbal reasoning to consciously digest the information gathered, one can make the desired choice to follow the active path of the direction chosen. It is this choice or decision one makes that keeps him or her acting in his or her lifestyle instead of just watching it go by. This is similar to my son's performance at the provincial gymnastic championships. He placed third one year, then second the following year however, the next year and he placed first! As noted in the movie *What the BLEEP Do We Know*, having the ability to be the *active participant* rather than just a *spectator* is key in always 'Moving Forward'!

Past discussions with my neurosurgeon indicated a similar theme and reflected the comment that "when people know better, they do better." Having the ability to think keeps the cognitive choice and the hope alive, and as we see in the book by Dr. Wayne Dyer, one can "choose, not excuse!" From a logical perspective, this seems easy—situations and decisions are either true or false, black or white, or yes or no. However, when we add emotional input into this equation, the emotional roller coaster begins. This emotional roller coaster can wreak havoc on one's inner self-worth. However, by simply choosing to focus on the positive aspects of one's thoughts or beliefs, one can reach his or her desired point. Again, we see a connection to the slogan "a belief is simply a thought I keep thinking," and we must realize that we can terminate this belief by choosing not to think that thought. This truly is a simple state of mind to obtain, and by doing so, we can get off the emotional roller coaster!

This is the same forward motion that my wife has chosen to pursue following a twenty-year hiatus in pursuing her dream of becoming a veterinarian. In her high school yearbook, it was noted under her grade-twelve graduation photo that her future occupation of choice would be a veterinarian. Here we see the interdependency that my wife shared with my independent career choice as a doctor then lawyer, working part time she chose to support me. Not unequivocally however as this was a time in her life when she desired having children, so by supporting me and working on a part-time basis, she also supported her desire for children. Working part-time allowed her the time flexibility to achieve this desired outcome as well as allow her to participate in her own personal wants and desires, such as cooking and engaging with her horses.

Ironically we now see a possible self-regarding theme to my wife's journey come into play with a comment she made re my current lifestyle role. Being very busy participating in one of her more 'time involved' vet school rotations, it appears that her time became seriously limited toward us; the family. Not totally but once again my involvement would be strongly required to meet our family's lifestyle need, i.e. competitive gymnastic training 4 days a week, swimming lessons 2 days a week, 3 cats, 2 dogs, groceries, school lunch and financial needs. Did she subconsciously discount my emotional challenge to this or was she biased from her past scholastic approach to things? Now I know, through the 'Law of Attraction' my energy was mirrored back to me through her. Just like the words said at our marriage, she was staying true to the wedding vows she made! Make no illusion, once again her energy kept me *'moving forward'*! ☺

Nevertheless, her entry into a graduate, related academic field proved very time consuming for me and with my emotional weakness perhaps this was too much for me to deal with. However as I have adapted so well to the past barriers presented before me this was just another road bump on my path. This reminded of the past comment my Neuro Surgeon made that "the better I get, the tougher it will become"! Here we see a possible challenge to the family gender role that traditional beliefs as well as society arguably support. After marriage, the novelty of the relationship wears off and after many years together the newness of dating is over. In North America when 2/3rds of couples divorce, people must choose an active investment role for each partner; active not speculative. I believe that is the fundamental issue couples need to willingly & consistently engage in.

This lifestyle expense has to be met or at the very least significantly offset. 'Balanced out' per say so one can intermittently get off the emotional roller coaster! Just like following the 3 'C's; more energy to Consciously & Consistently make a Choice! The needs of the many outweigh the needs of the few or the one and like Esther Hicks confirms, the "Law of Attraction will bring you what you want"[3] ! However as everything changes, we see a demographic shift away from the 'traditional family' stereotype as women now play a more active part in the social monopoly game. I too have 'changed' considerably however have learned to welcome this change! In my early recovery I found difficulty in altering my routine to now wanting these variations as they promote growth or the 'forward motion' we all need. Through reminders and notes, to smartphone agendas and a GPS, personal growth is my choice!

---

3   Esther & Jerry Hicks, The Teachings of Abraham: *The Vortex* (USA, Hay House Inc., 2009) A CD accompany to this book.

CHAPTER 6:

ADAPTATIONS

IN THIS NEXT section, we will discuss the term *adaptation*. The vocational counselor at the Nova Scotia Rehabilitation Hospital first introduced this term to me when I was a patient there. By using the word *adapt*, I was able to proactively find a way to achieve a desired result, and I felt as if I were participating in the process instead of simply reacting to it. I believe we all must adapt to the ever-changing environment we are involved in—the ever-changing environment called life! Playing the game of life is similar to playing a poker game, as people cannot choose what cards they are dealt but have to make the best hand with what they were given. Certainly the risk tolerances of different people will make them either bluff or end the game and fold; however, folding in this respect, when I am playing the game, is not an option.

Since this is individually my own life, I am on the front line—or, better yet, once again, the active participant and not just the spectator. Learning to adapt to the ever-changing environment we all face is something both motivation and inspiration support us through. However, ultimately, our conscious choice to move in the direction of reaching our desired goal is fundamentally selfish in nature. By expanding our circle of influence to be more than just ourselves—to include perhaps a life partner, a spouse, children, or even pets—this selfish choice becomes a selfless one. By using the term *adapt*, we gain a better understanding of the factors in this equation of life, because now it is not just a single, independent choice; it has become a multifaceted, interdependent one. There are certain pros and cons to this lifestyle that don't need to be addressed individually, as too much emphasis gets put on these factors. By following information gathered at the Hay House "I Can Do It!" conference that I went to last summer in Toronto, Ontario, guest speaker Dr. Wayne Dyer suggested one thing over everything else. To focus on the agenda at hand and process all the data but ultimately have *fun*!

It is this statement—to ultimately have fun—that I believe supports my wife's desire to reeducate herself to reach toward the top of the career pyramid and become a doctor of veterinary medicine. My wife's past experiences have prepared her for her pursuit of this goal—from working as a pet-care technician for a local veterinarian clinic, to moving to Florida to assist in opening a pet-care facility, to moving back to Canada to actively support my interests in finding another path to be very good at, to now achieving her own lifestyle ambition of becoming a veterinarian. Family adaptation to the lifestyle need we choose is the ultimate job at hand, and a major factor in the lifestyle equation is the social need or level that one has in it. It is this social level that weighs heavily on one's career choice. As I wanted to be very good at several things, having this lifestyle gave me the reward I was looking for—time and flexibility in my daily life—but made it less financially secure than obtaining a career.

What makes it more socially attractive having a career over a job? The social influence gains significant weight in one's lifestyle equation especially during public conversation with other individuals. As I said before this arena of individual performance is heavily influenced through marketing and social media. Over the years, I exceeded my expectations often on a personal job level that now I truly felt I found my lifestyle direction in the legal field. Achieving this professional status of becoming an attorney would give me the social advantage I wanted. However deep inside me nestled among my thoughts was an underlying belief in reducing the amount of social stimuli present to me; something a professional's lifestyle does not do! This is easily understood in this simple comment I made during the local newspaper's interview with me; "Live life don't let Life live you." (See Appendix B). It is this phrase for me that truly defines my basic, uncomplicated need to find balance in this life.

I made the comment again and again, "why don't you find a job while I stay home and support our family's lifestyle need as a "stay-at-home dad?" Ironically now because of this accident this theme is now being engaged some as I continue to adapt accordingly as I walk this new lifestyle path.

However, now as time goes on and I get older, the importance of being able to financially support myself when I'm old is very important to me. Selfishly it is just for me; however, selflessly it is for my entire family—or circle of friends, as my sister calls it. To support my older son's active level in gymnastics or my younger son's swimming experience, I need a positive lifestyle cash flow. It is this cash flow that my wife feels more active in providing than I do. Although not totally, the environmentally savvy energy I now feel focuses me more on the simplicity of playing life's game. The 'at one with nature' theme like those living a century ago attracts me. The idea of "divorcing society," just like George Carlin did in 1992, draws me in, but interdependently this is not easily attained.

It is not that I discount this lifestyle behavior; however, growing up, the features of living this way, and perhaps the materialistic needs I had, were socially simple. However, as time went on, elementary school turned into junior high, which then turned into high school, and the social wants increased as well. It was here that the lifestyle I was now living mirrored what the marketing companies focus their ads and strategies on. Not to discount it, but to simply address it, it was this socially influenced lifestyle that my wife grew up with in her early teen years.

For her, a family having two cars, an in-ground pool, a sauna, and vacations to destinations that included theme parks and ski resorts was normal. It was very different from my family. I came from a family where there were six children supported with one income, which made our lifestyle choices more limited from an income level—not boring but less financially savvy. Therefore, growing up as a child, my free time was spent being active outside—building tree houses, going fishing, hunting, and playing street games. In the winter, skating on the frozen ponds and sliding down the hills on a toboggan were activities of choice. In comparison, others with more disposable income may be spending free time downhill skiing, either locally or at ski resorts, or vacationing in a tropical environment.

The latter proves exciting to do; however, it was unrealistic to my upbringing. This reminds me of the slogan "Set your goals high and then exceed them," along with my adapted version of the same slogan: "Set your goals realistic and then achieve them." Achieving a goal allows one the reward of reaching the goal and actually feeling good instead of being disappointed or let down that the goal was not achieved. One can then set a destination in pursuit of another goal and do what is needed to achieve it. The latter of the slogans mentioned above fosters the same adaptive process I have shown my entire life—to systematically approach a desired goal, successfully achieve it, master it, and then adapt to something new. It is these levels of change I very much enjoy. Ironically, it is the same level of change that proved very disheartening to me early in my recovery. The multitasking and the processing of information required for this change were difficult processes to follow.

Relating back to simply being a spectator in life's game was a very rewarding and basic experience, as change did not exist for me. The concept of 'time' was at a standstill; each day felt like a Friday. However, now being an active participant, the same level proves to be simplistic and rather monotonous—so much so that the boredom I feel in performing this entry-level lifestyle requirement needs to be adapted to so that I feel the experience of moving forward. As everything has and always will change, it is inevitable that a person or business will do the same. By being an active player in life's game, we achieve this growth that best supports our adaptation to our ever-changing environment, and this growth refreshes the hope I hold on to.

However, a significant factor in this game is our gender roles. For these roles, either the man or the woman may have a traditional lifestyle theme. From the past scientific evolutionary standpoint, the man is responsible for certain things, while the woman is responsible for other things. However, as change is inevitable and as things will continue to change, here we see the social influence that gender roles have. From my personal perspective on growing up and gaining employment in the business world, I was fortunate enough to receive several supervisory roles where I had both a male and a female boss.

During these jobs, it was my personal preference to have a woman for a boss. I found a better balance of performance in meeting the business's needs when I had a supervisor of the opposite sex. Once again, we see the term *balance* come into play. To truly feel the best lifestyle steadiness, gender diversification worked well for me.

To add to this gender variation are the terms *feminist* and *chauvinist*. We see through past history that societies' guidance and influence were based heavily on patriarchal system. As time went on, women's entry into the business world became evident. Unlike twenty-five years ago, when men played a major factor in management roles, women now attain these positions readily. For some, this penetration into the business world justified their beliefs that a woman could compete with a man on a lateral playing field, performing the same job.

However, this belief escalated with the notion that a woman could perform better at the job at hand than the man, and the feminist movement was created. This is another example of how the universe operates through the law of attraction; society's feelings of chauvinism got offset, or attracted feminism.

As with chauvinism, I believe that feminism affects the lifestyle performance of all individuals. I also would argue that the women's movement to address society's male-dominated world is just as negative, if not more hurtful, to the family unit. It is this family unit that supersedes everything else when a man and a woman decide to bring children into the equation. In my own personal experience, through becoming more actively involved in my family's needs when my wife started school again, as hard as I tried, I fell short many times with my children's feelings. This was purely a biological response to a situation where traditional gender roles (i.e., the mother and the father) became interlaced. In the young mind, the executive-function portion of the brain is not developed yet, so this change proved irrelevant for my children. In most cases, the father's ability to actively be a part of the children's lives offers a unique perspective on the family unit. In a traditional family unit, the father is the worker/provider, while the mother is the nurturer/caregiver; yet here we see the roles beginning to reverse.

In a traditional family situation, the father can imitate the mother's approach to things; however, he can never duplicate it, because the motherly role in a family unit is unique. Because of this, women's entry into the business world affects the future lifestyle balance our children may carry forward. Time is the one constant we cannot control, and our children's morals and traditions will continue when our time has passed. Children's core beliefs hold significant weight for the future lifestyle of human beings; however, they get offset some by the current personality traits of the parents. It is the same traditional family traits or structure that a woman or Mom holds the key to with the family unit.

The top of any pyramid is the sharpest point of the structure, and a mother holds this same position. Instead of challenging chauvinism with feminism, women should realize that the true power they have is feminine grace. This lifestyle energy that a woman shows to her partner and children will not only better the way they see themselves, but also make better the energy given off to other people.

This relates to a comment that I often tell my sons: "for every action, there is a reaction." By keeping this in mind and by following the KISS theory (keep it simple, stupid), we fall back to our basic, or entry-level, standpoint. I have seen firsthand that when this energy is used, the family unit not only remains strong, but also adapts effectively as needed.

One response that came back from my earlier e-mail was from a very powerful person in my life. It appears that her childhood upbringing came from parents who broke the traditional value where the husband was the provider and the mother was the caregiver. Her mother was active in the workplace, pursuing her own individualized choice of being employed. At the time, she was raising two children, so one would think that the negative influences resulting from a lack of time spent in the mother-child role would somehow have impeded their development. Ironically, this was not the case.

The youngest daughter is an executive for Canada's largest bank, and the eldest daughter is the vice president of an insurance/finance company in Toronto, Ontario. This scenario, as rare as it may be, provides the same hope I hold on to and gives me the same energy I look to pass on to my two boys. In hindsight, it is obvious that these parents effectively managed the family need and passed on their positive guidance, which gave these two women positive energy. This positive energy in turn relates to their thoughts, which in turn relate to their beliefs and then ultimately their direction in life.

"As a belief is simply a thought we keep thinking"[4], we see here firsthand that positive energy attracts positive energy. Even though this family represents a small portion of society's population, they indeed offer the best representation of how a family unit should be. Kudos to them!

---

4   Esther & Jerry Hicks, The Teachings of Abraham: *The Vortex* (USA, Hay House Inc., 2009) A CD accompany to this book.

CHAPTER 7:

FINDING SELF-WORTH

As I said before, over the past decade of my life, I became very good at a handful of things but never truly excellent at one thing. The process of attaining perfection at the job at hand was very rewarding to me. However, once I was very good at it, I needed a new avenue or direction to follow. Ultimately, I think it is very important to find this inner lifestyle balance and focus all your effort and energy on reaching the desired level you want. I don't mean this in a bad way, but unfortunately for me, that funnel of direction was very big, so making streamlined choices was very rare.

By finding a more direct way to play life's game and by streamlining one's energy into a more specific lifestyle approach, one can find his or her own uniqueness. Some people come to realize this uniqueness at a very early age, while for others, like me, it can take a very long time. To understand one's drive, he or she must first know the reality of his or her choices. It is this reality that one's personality defines. Again, during my last appointment with my neurosurgeon, he offered the words "always hold on to the hope." It is this hope, or gray area, that I've always held on to, and it's the same hope that moves one in the forward-motion direction. However, some people have very analytical or logical personalities. Their character may indeed hold core morals and values; however, like adapting to one's physical role in their lifestyle (i.e., fat, thin, tall, or short), our mental attributes, or personalities are more difficult to change therefore can take precedent. In her academic journey, my wife had a personality test; it stated that she was of the green theme, which means she is quite logical and analytical. This is a very on-or-off, true-or-false, yes-or-no personality, and I believe the percentage of people like this found in society is small, restricting it's influence in the hopeful, gray, or maybe attitude.

As time is the one constant in the universe's equation, it can be argued that knowledge of where your lifestyle direction falls requires this time and that the contrast, as Esther Hicks calls it, provides you with better clarity before making a choice. On a résumé, both education and work experience play vital roles in creating a picture of that individual, because we know that work experience in a particular field correlates significantly to intelligence or knowledge in that same field. For this reason, finding true self-worth in some cases is a time-sensitive process, and, unfortunately, time is the only variable that cannot be controlled. From history books and past knowledge, we can learn how things were and can formulate thoughts about how they will be in the future; however, the fundamental real moment, or the eternal present, is the *now*! So even though time has progressed to whittle down the funnel of influence, the select jobs that people have entertained move them closer to their desired careers. I felt that all my jobs I was very good at would have been excellent at leading me down the path toward a career as a litigator!

Ultimately, finding a career is better than mastering a job. A career provides greater self-reward and offers a much more fulfilling lifestyle process than changing direction all the time. Just like we talked about earlier, lifestyle direction needs to correlate with a person's wants, both from society's influence and from the stimuli all around us. Human needs are quite simple: food, water, and shelter. However, because of society's influence, we see one's wants increase considerably. As discussed before, especially through holiday themes, social influence is a very powerful energy source, and this influence is introduced at a very young age through advertising campaigns, television commercials, and radio advertising. These ads are directed toward gaining the attention of a younger target market in hopes of attracting sales.

Early in my recovery, I would make monthly appointments with my psychologist to share my thoughts and ideas with a third-party individual outside of my family. I am certainly not discounting their efforts, but my family members probably, for emotional, religious, or domestic reasons, were biased in their direction of discussion. Talking with an educated, outside individual gave me another opinion that proved constructive to my learning process. Her unbiased view of my lifestyle role was very significant and meaningful to me. In my discussions with her, she supported some of my concerns but also debated with me and enlightened me on some. She helped me to realize I was looking outside of the lifestyle scope I was in. By understanding the lifestyle role I had to play, I was better able to recover and improve instead of attacking my thoughts, and I used that information to adapt and change the path I was on. This was a new lifestyle role for me—one that I needed to adapt to accordingly. It was here, early in my recovery, that I acted like a young child and shared the same learning curve with my son.

In one of my sessions with my psychologist, I brought my eldest son with me in hopes he would gain better insight into my lifestyle situation. As he was four years old when the accident happened, he basically had to handle what my other family members were experiencing. From dealing with my negative verbal outbursts to physically holding me up in the hospital bed so that I did not fall from it, the lifestyle level this young boy experienced was very demanding both physically and mentally. This was something that even mature adults had a difficult time with!

The comment "what doesn't kill you makes you stronger" often gets repeated in my head again and again, and this same knowledge applies to him. This episode will add significantly to his lifestyle experience and offer him future lifestyle rewards that he can draw from when needed. As the universal law of attraction affects everything, no matter how bad something is, going through this process makes me realize—and hopefully will make others realize too—that it can always be worse.

Because he experienced my early recovery as part of his developmental stage while growing up, we shared something. In discussions with my psychologist about the capacity we both had, at times I felt that my son's comments were rude and irritating. I came to realize that he did not yet have the upper cognitive functioning to make that choice. He was simply reacting to the environment the only way he knew how. Ironically for me, I too shared that developmental challenge.

Because the impact I received on my head damaged portions of my brain, particularly the frontal lobe, which is responsible for executive function, I also shared this upper cognitive deficit. However, as time continued on and my improvement slope remained positive, like my son, I too developed this higher-level process and began to understand my situation more clearly. We both developed this mind-set together and, like I stated before, will use this in our lifestyle process accordingly. This fact reminds me of one of NBC's past slogans: "and that's one to grow on." For me to personally adapt to this lifestyle role, my biggest challenge was the acceptance of this reality. Growing up, I often portrayed the character of a front-runner or leader in that I always wanted to lead the race or win. Also, I always wanted to do it my way; hence, the debate of character versus personality began. I believe character is something inherited through our genes, and personality is something we learn through our environment. My childhood environment was composed of the traditional family unit where the father was the provider and the mother was the caregiver and nurturer. This arrangement provides an equal balance to the family scale, but with society's influence, that has begun to change.

Because of my accident and the prior acceptance of my wife to our lifestyle, she now chose to become a much more independent and directed person, with all of the family's interests together. However, here we see a reversal of society's traditional gender roles and I feel this discord accordingly. In social events, often I am asked, "What do you do?" Falling back on my past entrepreneurial theme, at first I would reply that I was self-employed, that I was working when I had to, that I was the family manager, or that I was retired. To my surprise, when I started using the Mr. Mom theme, I was greeted with more enthusiasm and excitement than during my prior discussion attempts. Because I am able to spend the amount of time I do at forty-four years old with my children and actively support their lifestyle roles, I was often envied.

In conversations with these people, I gained a lot of positive energy from the jealousy they felt for my lifestyle role. Through society's eyes as well as academics, I envisioned a successful lifestyle correlated directly with a professional career or the acquisition of wealth. I had always thought that one had to be a doctor, a lawyer, or some other professional to feel grander in society's ranking and be in a position that others wished they could be in. However now without the time limits of a professional career, I am choosing to actively 'Live Life' not letting 'Life Live Me'!

CHAPTER 8:

BEING PROUD

IN THIS CHAPTER, I will discuss the phrase "being proud." I believe this phrase is difficult to digest, as being proud can sometimes lead to being conceited. By looking at your lifestyle experiences and digesting them to formulate a better understanding of your daily activities, you can hopefully look impartially at the overall person you are. As the sum of all the parts equals the whole, the individual choices you make snowball together to paint a better picture of the actions in your life, making you who you are.

Again, like I tell my son, "for every action, there is a reaction." Therefore, by remembering all your past actions, you can get a real understanding of the moment and feel proud of what you have achieved. It is then that you replace the term *conceited* with *confident*, and when that happens, self-praise, or feeling proud of yourself, follows. When I look at the past several years of my life, with all the barriers and obstacles that were present, it helps reassure me that my feelings of self-worth are ones, similar to those in a history book, that were made through my ability to adapt to an ever-changing environment. As I said before, this ability to adapt effectively is a very strong and powerful behavior that, when looked at collectively, can lead you to feel confident and proud in your actions.

Nevertheless, by feeling confident in our abilities, in addition to combating society's influence, we flirt with the gender role based on the defined, traditional family unit. Throughout history, the male gender has proven many times to be at the top of society's paradigm. From scientifically evaluating and researching new ideas to developing and inventing new items, societies have had largely patriarchal influences. However, in the past half century, the female introduction into the workforce has increased significantly. With that in mind, parts of this gender group have used their success in a feministic approach to contrast the once-chauvinistic arena. Instead of complementing each other, the male and female gender roles compete with each other. The energy and effort that gets shaped by this opposition gets wasted, as nothing constructive is ever really understood. That's not to say that a woman's entry into this marketplace is not challenging in itself, but focusing time, effort, and energy into this separate kind of movement takes away from the lifestyle balance a family, as well as a business unit, needs.

Ultimately, as said before, for me a woman's role in the marketplace provides a well-balanced atmosphere for the business unit. Instead of following a feminist approach, if women gave off a more constructive energy level, such as that found in feminine grace, their lifestyle and business needs would benefit significantly.

It is here that the feminist versus chauvinist debate begins. It is unfortunate that this confrontation exists, because finding the true business balance is lost. Instead of cooperation, we see competition, and instead of camaraderie, we see separatism.

Looking away from both of these business environments, one can get a better understanding of the business need. It is clarifying and understanding this desired outcome that ensures profitable sales and business growth. I believe that too much emphasis is placed on this gender-role debate in any business, as this is simply energy wasted. If this energy was redirected back into effectively pursuing the business need, obvious positive gains would exist.

Getting back into this feeling of pride, one can easily see that feeling proud relates to the positive energy that the individual or family unit can feel. During our early years of development, if we grow up in an environment filled with love and pride, we learn this behavior and mold it into our personality traits. These personality traits, combined with our characters, help us achieve the lifestyle balance we look for. Going back to my earlier comment about showing love, respect, and kindness, we see once again the comparison to respect, honesty, and having fun. There is no question that achieving your goal is a proud moment, and when you feel pride, you in turn are having fun. Consciously and consistently reminding yourself of your proud moments adds more "fun fuel" to your fire. Fire, in this respect, is a metaphor for hope, and the more often you feel this sensation of hope, through the law of attraction, you will draw forth positive energy. By doing this as often as you can, you stay on that moving-forward path!

Last week, when working on my manuscript for this book, I hit what is called writer's block. Unfortunately, during my manuscript-writing process, formulating my thoughts and ideas into written text was extremely difficult. In digesting the scenario and trying to figure out why my writer's block was happening, I came to the conclusion that I was not in a proper mental/physical balance. Today, following the same agenda and outline that I normally do in writing this manuscript, I followed my physical routine and exercised diligently to start my day off. Now, as I sit here after exercising and getting cleaned up, I find myself in a better frame of mind to put my thoughts on paper; hence, the manuscript writing process begins again.

Looking back at the outline of my past ideas, followed by a written agenda of each topic, I find myself in a better frame of mind to continue. As I reach the concluding chapter and the epilogue to this book, I feel reassured that staying in balance contributes significantly to moving forward for all of us. By staying in balance, as I call it, we are better able to play this poker game of life with the cards we're dealt. On that note, we will discuss ideas and methods to use in reaching the final destination of the journey: finding peace. The challenge that exists is that we are emotional beings, and feelings weigh heavily in our lifestyle choices. When feeling bad or having discontent with a particular feeling, a person's helpful natures kicks in because he or she does not like to feel that way. One then expends similar energy on making things right by giving peace and happiness to someone else. This is effort wasted as once again, this sense of purpose or feeling, simply boils down to the individual's choice, and one should not look outside him- or herself to find that purpose.

As one can see, my description of feeling proud carries more weight than the single or individual definition as my lifestyle attachment has more influence than simply a single choice. Since I made the decision to have a family, their opinions and interests are added into my lifestyle equation. Looking at myself on an individual basis and seeing all of the barriers and obstacles I overcame, as hard as it was at times, instead of choosing to give up or stop, I chose to actively continue on rebuilding my life! Active participation is key to feeling proud so once I achieved the realistic goal I set, I felt the immediate reward of success. Feeling this emotion strengthened my determination to continue moving on this lifestyle path, overcoming the smallest to largest difficulties that came up.

Fundamentally, I believe that excitement will always exist; however, true happiness is not the same. As seen time and time again, even in very difficult lifestyle positions (for example, some people are put in jail), lifestyle harmony can exist. These people make the choice, as their environments cannot change, to find peace and contentment with their situations. However, I believe that when a choice to move is available, finding this contentment can be very difficult to do. Therefore, a direct correlation exists between one's environment and his or her level of happiness. Finding 'peace' or 'purpose' in life's journey is one's ultimate goal!

CHAPTER 9:

REFLECTION AND CHOICES

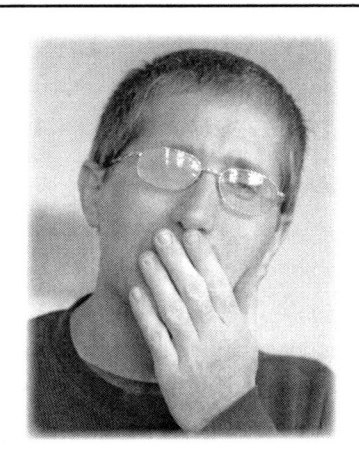

IN THIS CHAPTER, I will discuss themes and identify visions that truly embrace the individual choice. As discussed previously, it is the individual's choice that is at the top of the lifestyle pyramid, and it is this choice that boils down to the individual's sense of comfort. If one is comfortable, then fundamentally one's lifestyle feels in balance, as he or she is at peace, or has contentment with life's daily flow. However, as high-impact or intense moments like the one I experienced happen, we all need to proactively have a reserve supply of coping energy to deal with these events.

By having this supply of energy, we put ourselves in a better position to handle the ever-changing environment we live in, so when these moments happen, we are not only prepared for them but also, more importantly, ready for them to happen.

To expect the unexpected is the ideal, but to be ready for the unexpected is not only more effective and efficient but also proactively more secure. It is this sense of security that recharges and reenergizes our lifestyle batteries to help us keep walking on this path. To give up or walk off this path supports the negative energy so many of us easily succumb to. When these moments of weakness arrive, we must again, always adapt and simply change the direction of our motion.

Like Anthony Robbins says, staying in motion helps our emotions! I want to say this again in order to stress its significance: staying in motion is the one absolute, or the one fundamental, that everyone must push for. When we are inactive or static, the negative vortex of energy starts building with thoughts, then feelings, and then performance. Ultimately, negative changes in our performance result in negative changes to our life!

Keeping the slope of your lifestyle positive or above zero, logically directs you to choose not to plateau hence are always moving forward. Once the point of lifestyle comfort is reached, simply maintaining and supporting this lifestyle foundation is key. By truly accepting the position we have reached, we have attained peace. Now we can truly live the lifestyle we choose to live or move forward again. I believe that so much energy is wasted reacting to certain events. By using this same energy in a more constructive and proactive measure, we are truly able to adapt our lifestyle focus in order to reach the next resting point. In the same way, on major interstate highways in the

United States, rest areas are geographically placed to allow drivers to recharge their energy back into their driving style.

This is very similar to an individual walking on his or her lifestyle path. A good night's sleep enables us to start each day with a well-rested and balanced mind, and so does sporadically resting or reenergizing when needed. Some cultures use this idea heavily in the form of socialized breaks or mandatory siestas. Very similar to a workweek where Sunday is considered the day of rest, having a systematic break in the lifestyle workflow is key to establishing the mental/physical balance. Per the universal law of attraction, the energy recuperated during these breaks not only makes an individual more productive, but also attracts positive energy. To start my day with positive thoughts, I placed a note in my vanity drawer where my toothbrush was so each morning I would be directed to it. This note listed the '10 reasons why I Love my Life' and each day I would choose not to just simply read it, but do so in front of the bathroom mirror. I could then look directly into my eyes while I read it so I could truly feel a visual sense of this & start my day feeling good!

It is a win-win-win situation when the energy recovered then gets used for achieving a greater good for society's collective.

CHAPTER 10:

HOLD ON TO THE HOPE

IN THIS CHAPTER, I'll discuss the term *hope*. How does one define hope? Does it even exist? In the preface of this book, the definition of *hope* as per www.dictionary.com states, "*the feeling that what is wanted can be had or that events will turn out for the best*". It is this element that defies one's logical stream of input in making a decision. All of the yes or no, the black or white, and the true or false get pushed aside, as they leave no room for the gray area, or the maybe. It is this gray area that provides the energy to one's hopeful nature regarding possible results. It is the same adaptive process that I followed early in my recovery when traditional medicine stated that my recovery "might be as good as it gets." I still follow this energy now that I'm closer to the total-recovery level.

As said before, simply reaching the desired destination point for a particular goal—or, in life, growing old and getting closer to one's death—does not foster the gratification of reaching that goal. Going through the journey and getting there is the reward. Early in my recovery, I had a discussion with my eldest brother regarding my lifestyle performance, and he made me understand without any skepticism that the road to peace is a bumpy path. As stated in the movie *The Vow*, it is these "moments of impact or high intensity that end up defining who we are." In that respect, the following moment occurred. Early in my recovery, while I was still in a coma in the hospital, it was either a chemical reaction in my brain from the trauma I received or a real experience I had with my deceased mother.

Once the medication I was receiving to keep me in the medically induced coma was stopped, I was to wake up; but four days later, I still had not. During this time, I experienced a brief, high-level moment with my deceased mother. In this moment, she instructed me that "It's time to get up; you're not ready yet." Ironically, the next day I did wake up. This episode was very similar to the e-mail correspondence I received from that gentleman who told me "to keep in contact with your angels and guides as they are there to help you with everything that you do." Indeed, defying logic and science, I was assisted or safeguarded by my mother's energy!

The years since my mother's death have shown me that my actions are being protected or secured somehow so that negative situations are never as severe as they could be. I have always been shielded, so to speak, so I truly believe my guardian angel is one of pure and absolute energy—my mother.

Theresa Caputo's work on the *Long Island Medium* supports this claim; however, until my thoughts or memories get validated somehow, my feelings are the only real avenue to follow. With such a long timeframe, over 2+ years, I have put my name on her waiting list. Hopefully a future connection with her will happen and the others in my family, especially my father, will get validated!? For me, I have that validation already! Neither structured religion nor denominational faith can compete with the simple spiritual flow or the vibrational energy the universe has!

Unfortunately, science revolves around what it can prove or justify and is strictly logical, making it a limited means with which to view life—powerful and specific but restricted as well. Now with the extent of scientific proof, the largest realm in our belief is the 'Universe'. Like centuries ago when the world was believed to be flat, further evidence proved it was not. In that respect, as the limit of our Universe is understood, we are starting to see theories that other Universes' exist. In time another definition of it's vastness will be quantified.

CHAPTER 11:

ATTAINING PEACE

ATTAINING PEACE, OR obtaining a lifestyle that directs positive energy to you, is indeed a lifestyle that is absolute. In order to deal with social agendas and not succumb to the advertising and marketing influence that big businesses have on people, people need to truly identify and live by their core values in order to reach a level of contentment. Growing up as the youngest of six children and part of a family whose income was supplied by one source, my father, I had my introduction to the status quo of society's sway early in life, especially when high school hit!

I believe this power, or social energy force, restrained the lifestyle direction I was on, especially when compared to those who had more social etiquette, as my wife calls it. At a young age, respect for life always played a part in my actions—so much so that enjoying nature's beauty early in the morning while I went hunting far exceeded the disruption that came after killing an animal—a partridge, no less. For me, I was very glad it was not a bigger and more significant kill like a deer!

As written before, like in the movie *The Vow*, this accents a comment made by the husband in that movie: "There are moments of impact and high intensity that end up defining who we are." My accident indeed was a "moment of impact" and was of high intensity for me. However, just as acts of war have manipulated social influence, my accident gave me a better respect for life. It is this respect that allows me to keep environmental impact at the top of my lifestyle pyramid—a feeling that moves me down an energy-efficient path that focuses on conserving and reducing.

To reduce, reuse, and recycle is more important than to live effectively. Living in a city brings effectiveness, but one needs to live efficiently as well. On my recent trip to Malibu, California, a state that has a population on par with Canada, I gained energy from the brother of the gentleman who opened his "resort of a house" to us for the New Year's Eve celebration. The brother of this gentleman chose a Toyota Prius as his car of choice. As gasoline is formed from a fossil fuel, this hybrid car reduces his carbon footprint on the environment. It is this reduction that fosters the environmental saviness I have and attracts my holistic lifestyle approach.

Unfortunately, living in a city can affect the environmental impact one makes. By not driving a car each day, and instead walking to acquire essentials, one thinks his or her carbon footprint is smaller because of reduced gasoline consumption. Living outside the city, one must drive each day to access the same essentials. However, for myself, living in the city now and driving my children to and from school each day shows me firsthand that the amount of gas I burn is higher now than when we lived outside the city on a school-bus route.

❦

A bus has advantage over one's personal car, as it holds over twenty-five-plus students, whereas my car simply holds two. Some carpool parking lots foster this same advantage for other individuals traveling to and from work from outside the city.

To find the best balance between rural living and city living, one can enjoy the benefits of a suburban life. As highway driving is more efficient than city driving, gas consumption should remain the same, with a chance to be even less. Living outside the city allows one to also engage in green energy resources (e.g., a solar boiler to supply heat to your home, a windmill, or photoelectric cells). Here we see a reduction, if not elimination, of the combustion of fossil fuels to generate heat; instead, the energy provided is free and clean, coming directly from the sun.

Understanding one's core values and beliefs is key in attaining peace and finding balance in the lifestyle one chooses to live. It is this balance that gives one a sense of worthiness, and living a lifestyle this way can be passed on to other generations. My children will know firsthand how to live a life not only through love and kindness, but also, more importantly, through respect, honor, and having fun. Eroding away our environment by choosing not to actively live in a way that supports it is in no way considerate or fun! Choosing to live in an environmentally conscious way redirects my energy to others and truly expresses a sense of immortality!

Unfortunately, living in the city can mislead one; ultimately, it's a lifestyle that's convenient rather than necessary. Our focus on environmental impact, especially for the sake of future generations, is not only our responsibility but also a necessity. As I said before, for every action, there is a reaction, so we must take an active and consistent approach toward investing in our future generation and be as environmentally savvy as we can be. By doing this and living this way, we can truly find contentment and attain the peace we seek. However, this choice is debatable, and not everyone makes this choice. To some, ignorance is bliss!

Epilogue

One thing that has stimulated me on the recovery path has been the universal law of attraction, which maintains that positive energy attracts positive energy. This energy can arguably be applied to positive thoughts, which in turn lead to positive feelings and ultimately to a lifestyle direction or path guided by the universe's energy source.

This energy source, for me, is not limited by mankind's depiction in any organized religious foundation. Because I was born in North America, my lifestyle was sheltered from eastern European and Asian beliefs. Christianity was a learned tradition I experienced during my upbringing. I don't mean to discount it or any other capital-*R* religion; however, following a belief that mankind created not only limits the amount of data used also but narrows the funnel of this universal energy.

From a scientific standpoint, and for me, one absolute that exists above all others is that the universe controls—or, rather, adapts and influences—everything!

I think it's important to understand the quality of one's lifestyle. Ironically, talking with my eldest son over lunch, the topic of environmental friendliness came up. When we look at all the conveniences that have been invented over the past fifty years, we tend to forget the simplicity of our environment and the complexity of nature. To reduce, reuse, and recycle is an important way of life, but this way gets challenged on a daily basis by what we choose to do for the sake of convenience, regardless of wastefulness (for example, consider taking a bus versus driving a car versus riding a bike). Efficiencies often get replaced with conveniences.

Getting back to the theme of being at one with nature, we are easily misled into abusing the one absolute that is so real: our environment. This morning while taking my shower, I made the conscious and deliberate choice to turn the water off while I soaped up and washed myself. By doing this, I passed energy on and respected my environment by not wasting water and heat energy. Putting access to water in perspective is very important to my sister, who performs contract works in Bermuda, where water is not readily available. The environment does not support the drilling of a well, as the land was formed by volcanoes and lava—hence, no soil levels.

It is common for homes there to utilize a cistern water system in which the rain gutters and eaves troughs are directed into a large storage bin. That water that nature created via rain can then be used for washing dishes, showering, and even flushing the toilet, where water cleanliness is not important. Drinking water is either purchased separately or a water filtration system is used. This kind of environmental maintenance is similar to the relationship support that I discussed previously.

On a simple basis, because we are at one with nature, we can transfer the same energy into being at one with our relationship. I believe living a lifestyle this way has a direct effect on the young minds growing up around me, my two sons.

As previously discussed, it is clear that we need to take ownership of the environment that we live in. Depending on where—and, more importantly, how—we grew up, we took advantage of the modernizations that had been created. By truly putting this energy toward our environmental base, we live not only effectively but also, more important, efficiently! Business and personal changes are inevitable; however, growth is an option, a choice we all must energetically make!

To love others, people must love themselves first, and to love nature, people must not only love themselves first but also, more importantly, have love for the others who will come after them. As our lives on this planet are mere grains of sand on a beach, one day we will no longer exist; however, for those who make the choice to have a family, their children will continue on when they die. With this basic yet creative foundation in their minds, future generations will be further ahead of the collective mind-set that society and marketing have created.

This is a prime directive of the "always adapt" theme I talk about, as an informed mind is a powerful mind. In relation to this theme and the title of this book, *Moving Forward*, is also a lifestyle adaptation in progress. If we choose to continually challenge ourselves and extend effort outside of our comfort zone, we follow the ever-changing process of always moving forward. With the onslaught of marketing and money spent on advertising, it is difficult for one to remain individually focused on the simplicities of life and truly follow a lifestyle that focuses on the same.

We not only receive the negative energy brought on by these materialistic paradigms but also feel it as our circle of influence becomes larger with friends. My children often compare their lifestyles with things their friends have and the rules their friends get to live by. They then cast negative energy toward my wife and I, as our family rules seem unfair. Here we see that we are not only affected by what our parents teach us but also influenced by our friends and what their parents teach them.

To compete in this respect is not an option; therefore, the circle of influence that I choose to use is simply my immediate family and some very close friends. In comparison, the other 7+ billion people on the planet can collectively or independently gather their own information and have their own thoughts and feelings to ultimately make their own individual choices. The greatest benefit this injury gave me was the ability to start this life all over again—blank and clean, so to speak.

Again, as quoted from a past e-mail response to me, "I have been given the option of living a life unfettered by old memories." I can now simply focus on the direct effects of my actions. My actions will affect my environment, but, more importantly, they will affect my family and me! When my time is up on this planet, my last thought will be "Live life; don't let life live you!" Too many people get caught in society's menagerie of wants and never really live their lives free from obstructed marketing views, as these views are frequently found with their family, friends, or neighbours.

Similar to what George Carlin did in 1992, "a divorce of society" may prove beneficial. By removing this influential energy source, people can possibly find the satisfaction or contentment they seek and live lifestyles that benefit or uphold the good of the environment!

In closing, I'd like to share two photos of myself—one taken the summer one year before my accident, at a NASCAR race in Bristol, Tennessee, and one taken three years later. The benefits of starting life all over again and losing forty-five pounds from muscle atrophy and my diet were solidified with the immediate physical reward I felt when at the beach! Starting early in my physical recovery and focusing on the 'forward motion' I always adapted to, I have learned with absolute certainty, the physical reward of living an active lifestyle!

The benefits of being an active participant in life's game and choosing to live a healthy and active lifestyle are evident. With 75 percent of the North American population challenged with their weight, I welcome this change! I will now work on and exercise my mental strength and my family connection to truly get my life more stable and secure—in balance, so to speak!

Unfortunately, I have deficiencies that no matter how hard I try to adjust or modify, they will not improve. The fine motor skills, i.e. hand writing, the balance and Vertigo issue I have will always be a deficit for me to deal with. Although, from advances with my right side arm movement, to leg and foot control, to the eventual semi-normal bipedal walking, these physical limitations I have successfully adapted to or overcame! Now however I am hopeful that establishing new neural pathways still exist and after reading Dr. Norman Dodge's book [5], The Brain that Changes Itself, I am confident and optimistic that I will continue to keep "Moving Forward"! With that in mind I will 'always-adapt' and welcome whatever change may come! I symbolize the other 'AA' ☺

---

5   Norman Dodge, M.D.,The Brain that Changes Itself (USA, Viking Penguin Group Inc. 2007)

http://youtu.be/ztfkhdYFiPY

Be *motivated* all you like, and be *inspired* even more; however, if you are not *determined* and you rely only on sheer fortuitous luck, your goals will never happen!

When it is all said and done, for me, knowing firsthand that total recovery can never truly be an option, I leave you with the following. My behavior has changed from what or how it used to be, but my character remains intact. With the solid morals and values passed on to me from my parents and upbringing, my choice now is to actively adjust to my ever-changing environment! I will continue to adjust to this game called life, constantly learning, adapting, and having fun while walking this path. Instead of being happy all the time, I am truly grateful for everything life has given me, even my accident for it has given me a perspective that could not be realized any other way! Knowing that 'moments of weakness' or change will always happen, I will fearlessly continue to play this game called life! To be grateful all the time, one doesn't need excitement they just need to simply make the choice!

As the old saying goes "everything happens for a reason" so I believe this accident was dealt to me to add to the lifestyle commitment I talk about. Through the power of positive energy and that of my deceased mother I conclude the following. Like a book my sister in law gave me, "The Purpose Driven Life"[6], educating others to the source energy the Universe has is now the path I am on! By continually "Moving Forward" and knowing negative energy sources will often deprave your lifestyle energy, I determinedly now know that each and everyone of us will always and forever succeed! Rest easy, everyone. Breathe, relax, and smile often!

Best to all, and like Dr. Wayne Dyer says, "Choose, don't excuse!" Follow my lead, and do like me; make the choice, and do whatever it takes! Always believe in yourself!

Be well.

---

6   Rick Waren, The Purpose-Driven Life, (USA Zondervan, 2002)

APPENDIX A

Paraphrase from Neuro Psyche Report

Date of Assessment, April 1, 2009

"Mr. Gillis sustained traumatic brain injury (TBI) after the motorcycle he was driving was struck by a car. He was assigned a Glasgow Coma Scale of 3 by Emergency Personnel there, (suggestive of a severe TBI) and transferred by ambulance to the Hospital Emergency Room. ER personal there noted multiple rib fractures, a liver contusion, a ruptured spleen, and a bilateral pneumothorax or two punctured lungs and a CT scan revealed a left parietal hemorrhage. He was later transferred to the Nova Scotia Rehabilitation Hospital where he was found to be confused with reduced right body movement and sensation. He also had symptoms of right field neglect, decreased motor planning, left/right confusion, diplopia or double vision and memory difficulties as well as language related difficulties.

GCS score VS Mortality %

3 (That was ME!!)	65
4	45
5	35
6	24
7-13	10 -15

www.braintrauma.org/pdf/protected/prognosis_guidelines.pdf
(pg. 164.)

Appendix B

Number of document(s): 4
Creation date: **January 6, 2011**

The Chronicle-Herald
The Chronicle-Herald
Front, Friday, December 9, 2005. p. A1

Awakening to life's gifts; Brain-injured and in a coma for six long weeks, young dad blessed with miraculous second chance

Jennifer Stewart Staff Reporter

Live life, don't let life live you.

That's Wayne Gillis's new philosophy, he said Thursday, as he struggles to rebuild the pieces of his life that were snatched away by a brain injury three months ago.

"I love you, sweetie," Wayne whispers to Lisa, his wife of 10 years. Behind his glasses, tears spring to his eyes.

"I love you too," she replies, leaning forward to share a kiss.

The couple, who own a farm in Shubenacadie, have had a rough go since Wayne's motorcycle accident on Sept. 7. But things started to look up in early November when the 36-year-old father of two awoke from a six-week coma.

Since then, he's been recovering steadily with the help of the caring staff at the Nova Scotia Rehabilitation Centre in Halifax.

Wayne says he remembers nothing of the crash, which happened on Highway 2 near Lantz.

"I just answered the phone, had to go fix a computer, got on my bike and away I go," he said, gesturing with his hands. "The next thing I know I'm in this place, waking up in here."

"Life just goes on."

Lisa, a tiny blond with pretty features, looks on quietly.

"We are truly blessed to have Wayne recover so well," she said, her blue eyes wide and shining.

"That was the worst day I've ever had, getting that phone call when he had the accident and then just seeing him in the hospital and not knowing if he'll pull through it."

Looking back, she said she never could have made it without the love and support of "so many people."

"Our friends, our family, people that we don't even know," Lisa said. "All the prayers and generosity and just people calling and saying 'Can we do anything?' That's given me strength to give him the strength to get through it."

She said she was especially surprised by the response of the biker community. Led by East Coast Riders and novascotiabikers.com, motorcycle enthusiasts raised $13,000 for the family through a poker run in October.

"That strength, that's really, really important," Wayne said. "That means something real."

He smiled at his wife, who reached over and slipped her slender hand inside his.

"Things that are real, and stuff that I can see and feel and touch, those are the things that mean something to me," he said. "Children, family and friends. I can see them, obviously I can touch them, and they can relate with me."

Behind them, Samuel, 4½, dashed across the room, clattering a giant plastic candy cane on the tiled floor. Gladwin Buckler watched his eldest grandson while he wheeled six-month-old Matthew in a tiny stroller. The infant squealed happily, slapping his sock feet together.

"That was the worst afternoon, when that one doctor said that's as good as he's going to get," he said, describing his son-in-law lying-in a hospital bed, full of tubes.

"He was basically a vegetable then. It was terrible."

Gladwin flew in from Florida five weeks ago to help his daughter, who was trucking the children back and forth to Halifax almost daily.

He says it's unbelievable how far Wayne has come, although he knows he still has a way to go yet.

"They said it will take probably nine months to a year," Gladwin said.

When he first arrived at the rehab centre, Wayne underwent a series of tests to determine the level of his motor and communication skills. At the time, out of a possible 56 points, Wayne managed a four.

a solution from **CEDROM SNi**

85

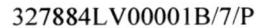